CLASSIC ROCK
NUMBER 07

DEVILS TOWER
WYOMING

AND

THE BLACK HILLS
SOUTH DAKOTA

by
John Harlin III

FALCON®

CHOCKSTONE®

A FALCON GUIDE®

Falcon® Publishing is continually expanding its list of recreation guidebooks. All books include detailed descriptions, accurate maps, and all the information necessary for enjoyable trips. You can order extra copies of this book and get information and prices for other Falcon® books by writing Falcon, P.O. Box 1718, Helena, MT 59624 or calling toll-free 1-800-582-2665. Also, please ask for a free copy of our current catalog. Visit our website at www.Falcon.com or contact us by email at falcon@falcon.com.

ISBN: 1-57540-025-1 *Classic Rock Climbs* series
    1-57540-028-6 *Devils Tower Wyoming and The Black Hills, South Dakota*

Falcon, FalconGuide, and Chockstone are registered trademarks of Falcon Publishing, Inc.

Cover photo by Bob Gaines.
All uncredited photos by John Harlin III.

Cataloging-in-Publication data on file at the Library of Congress.

FOREWORD

This booklet springs, phoenix-like, from a vastly larger three-volume tome I wrote a decade ago, *The Climber's Guide to North America*. Crisscrossing the continent to explore fifty-or-so climbing areas, I sometimes could hardly contain my joy. How could a climber get so lucky as to earn a modest living while seeing new sights and feeling the distinctive touch of more kinds of rock than most of us get to jam and pinch in a lifetime? At the time I thought I could always spare a few months to go on a road trip to update new editions of *The Climber's Guide*. But life has a way of growing complicated, and when the time came for bringing these chapters up to date for the new *Classic Rock Climbs* series, I enlisted the capable help of Dave and Annie Getchell, who had the pleasure of loading their pickup truck with climbing gear and striking off for new horizons. They contributed the information for climbing in Mt. Rushmore National Monument, a place where no one climbed 14 years ago when I first visited the Black Hills. But neither they nor I did our "work" in a vacuum. Vital information was also contributed by Bob Archbold, Mike Engle, Dennis Horning, Andy Petefish and Paul Piana, to whom we'd like to extend our sincere gratitude for helping to make our work more useful and accurate. No doubt errors have still chimneyed their way into this book, and for those I must accept full responsibility. To all users of this book I wish many fine days of climbing. But most of all, I wish you all the joys that come with fresh discoveries in two of the most beautiful places in the world.

—John Harlin

TABLE OF CONTENTS

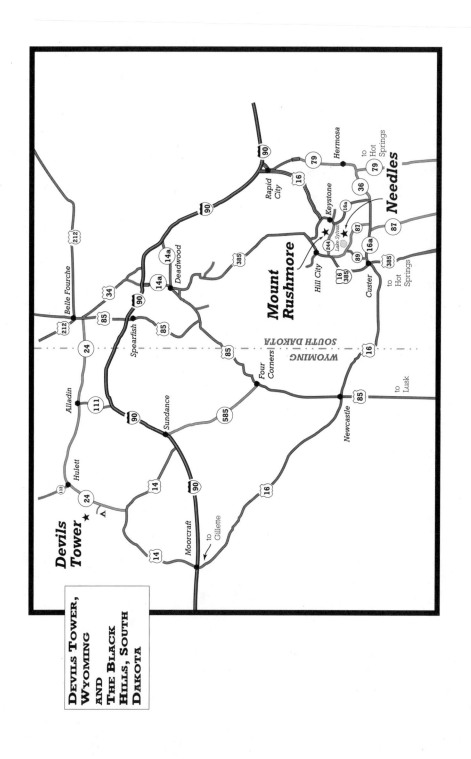

Devils Tower, Wyoming AND The Black Hills, South Dakota

INTRODUCTION

DEVILS TOWER, WYOMING and THE BLACK HILLS, SOUTH DAKOTA

by John Harlin III

Devils Tower and the Black Hills lie in two states and would seem to occupy different planets as far as the landscape and the climbing are concerned, yet they are only 70 air-miles apart. Each is equally magnificent and a visitor has done himself a real disservice if he only visits one area and not the other.

SELECTION OF ROUTES   The routes chosen here provide a full sampling of top-quality climbing in each area. While the route selection attempts to cover most of the better routes at these areas, not all will be considered "classic." Sometimes, especially in the easier grades, lesser routes were included to provide options for climbing at a particular level. Some genuinely classic lines may have been excluded due to layout considerations.

ROUTE DESCRIPTIONS   Most of the route descriptions follow a series of dots placed over photographs. Notations of difficulty, fixed protection and belays appear along the route lines. This book is only a guide. The lines on the photographs merely approximate the actual climbs; route-finding skills are an absolute necessity.

Assume that the listed protection is in addition to a clean (no pitons) rack with one piece from each of the standard size increments from ¼-inch to 2½ inches.

Unless they are listed in the guidebook, or needed in emergency situations, *pitons or bolts should never be placed on established routes!*

RATINGS   North American climbers use a combination of four rating systems for assessing difficulty. The first is a rough classification of the various stages from trail hiking to aid climbing. The next system breaks the technical free-climbing down into specific decimal ratings that form the mainstay of American rock-climbing ratings, and refer to the hardest individual free moves. Sometimes an overall route rating will be raised somewhat if the climbing difficulty is extremely continuous, but not always.

Rarely does a lack of protection affect the free rating of a climb; instead, protection considerations are mentioned more as a footnote to the grade. Typically, an "R" protection suffix denotes considerable runouts between available protection, with the potential for serious injury in case of a fall.

Aid climbing is also differentiated into various degrees of difficulty; seriousness is a part of the rating.

Additionally, many routes are given a Roman numeral grade to indicate their length. Thus, an example of an overall route rating might be VI 5.10 A3. Individual pitches might be labeled 5.6, 4th, 5.10R, or A2. An explanation of each category follows.

Class Description

- Class 1: Trail hiking.
- Class 2: Rough hiking, frequent use of hands for balance.
- Class 3 (often abbreviated as 3rd): Scrambling over rock using hands, sometimes exposed enough so inexperienced climbers prefer the security of a rope.
- Class 4 (or 4th): Technically more difficult; most climbers use a rope and belay, but don't place protection.
- Class 5 (or 5th): Free climbing sufficiently difficult to require a rope and protection placements for safety.
- Class 6: Artificial (aid) climbing, where hardware serves not only for protection, but also for hand- and footholds.

Fifth-class climbing is subdivided into decimal grades from 5.0 on up. Currently, the most difficult climbs are in the 5.14 category. Routes 5.10 or

International Rating Systems Compared

West German	YDS	British	Australian	East German	French
	5.0				
	5.1				
	5.2				
	5.3				
	5.4				
	5.5				
	5.6				
5+	5.7	4b · VS		VIIa	5a
6-	5.8	4c	15	VIIb	5b
			16		
6	5.9	HVS	17		5c
6+	5.10a	5a	18	VIIc	6a
7-	5.10b	5b · E1	19	VIIIa	6a+
7	5.10c		20	VIIIb	6b
	5.10d	E2	21	VIIIc	6b+
7+	5.11a	5c		IXa	6c
8-	5.11b	E3	22		
8	5.11c		23	IXb	6c+
8+	5.11d	6a · E4	24	IXc	7a
9-	5.12a		25	Xa	7a+
9	5.12b	6b	26	Xb	7b
	5.12c	E5	27		7b+
9+	5.12d		28	Xc	7c
10-	5.13a	6c · E6			7c+
10	5.13b	7a	29		8a
	5.13c		30		8a+
10+	5.13d	E7	31		8b
11-	5.14a		32		8b+

harder are broken down into further shades of difficulty with letter grades
(a, b, c, or d) or + and – signs.

Aid ratings reflect the security of using the latest available equipment. Most
current aid routes, if climbed with 1960s-era pitons instead of a modern aid
rack, would require an entirely different rating. Frequently, difficult nailups
simply couldn't be done without the technology of camming devices,
bashies and hooks.

- A1: Easy placements, completely secure.
- A2: More difficult placements, less secure, awkward moves.
- A3: Even more difficult or awkward placements that might only hold a
  short fall.
- A4: Placement might hold body weight, but would not sustain a fall.
- A5: Enough A4 placements strung together to risk at least a 50-foot fall
  should one fail.

Aid-rating prefixes like C1, C2, etc., indicate the rating when the route can
be done completely clean (i.e., with no hammer blows).

**WARNING ON ROUTE LINES, SYMBOLS AND FIXED
PROTECTION**   The format for most of the route descriptions in this
book—lines superimposed on photographs—is helpful only if one keeps in
mind the inherent imprecision of route information. The placement of route
lines or protection/belay symbols is not exact. The notations are subject to
on-the-spot interpretation, so routefinding skills remain just as important as
ever. The symbols and route lines are guides only.

There are bound to be ways to improve the route lines or topos. Reader
suggestions for corrected descriptions is invaluable in updating this book.
A photocopy of a picture from this book with corrections to the route is
ideal. Likewise, input concerning the route selection is appreciated, and
suggestions for better routes are always welcomed. Send route
information, corrections and suggestions to *Classic Devil's Tower and Black
Hills*, Chockstone Press, PO Box 3505, Evergreen, CO 80437-3505.

As further warning, be aware that fixed pitons and bolts labeled in this
guide might have been removed or supplemented since publication.
Always inspect fixed anchors carefully; they may be weak due to
weathering, poor initial placement or any number of reasons. That they are
listed here does not imply that they are trustworthy or even exist! Where
not considered necessary for routefinding, known fixed protection often has
been left out of the description.

Never trust a fixed piton without testing it first, preferably with a hammer.
Since few people free-climb with a hammer these days, fixed pins are
rarely tested and can easily be unsafe. Check bolts with a strong jerk on the

hanger (using a carabiner); inspect the hanger for cracks, and look closely at the surrounding rock for deterioration. Bolts should *never* be tested with a hammer, as this can severely weaken them! Because defective or poorly-placed bolts are a possibility anywhere, no single bolt can be fully trusted.

A NOTE ON SAFETY   Those using this guidebook are assumed to be competent, experienced climbers. It is not the intent of this book to educate anyone on *how* to climb, but simply to provide suggestions as to where to climb and a general sense of what the climbing will be like in a particular area.

It must be noted, however, that routes are relatively remote. Assistance from fellow climbers, rescues or hospital facilities may be difficult to obtain quickly. This should be a serious consideration before deciding just how far to "hang it out" on a particular climb.

Water sanitation is a problem in some areas. Beware that few streams and lakes are completely safe from contamination, no matter how far away from civilization. The bacteria giardia is a common infectious agent and can produce extreme intestinal ills that will completely ruin a climbing vacation. It is best to treat all stream or lake water with purification tablets, filtering or boiling. To avoid further water contamination, bury all human waste at least 100 feet away from the nearest open water.

Theft is an expensive problem in some areas, particularly those frequented by large numbers of people. As a general rule, keep all valuables, including climbing equipment, locked out of sight in a car. Ropes and equipment left fixed on routes, or stashed at the base of cliffs, may not be safe.

SECTION ONE

DEVILS TOWER, WYOMING

Rising abruptly out of the surrounding plains and forest, Devils Tower is so spectacular that it became America's first national monument. Its summit rises 900 feet higher than the encircling tourist-jammed trail; the final 500 feet are uniformly sheer. The columnar structure of this superb rock (phonolit porphyry) provides delightfully consistent crack-cranking on fissures of all sizes and difficulties. Because cliffs encircle the entire Tower, climbers can seek out or avoid the sun at their pleasure, rendering pleasant climbing almost year-round.

CLIMBING   Devils Tower formed as an ancient volcanic neck cooled into almost perfect hexagonal columns. Granite-like, but even harder, the rock is split by hundreds of vertical cracks that run the entire height of the face. On the south face, routes climb less than 300 feet before reaching the Meadows, a large bushy ledge from which vigorous third-classing leads to the top. The other faces rise a near-vertical 500 feet to the summit plateau.

As the surrounding landscape eroded away, the Tower's emergence hesitated for a few millennia about a third of the way from the summit. Because this section was exposed to the elements longer, it is somewhat more decomposed than the perfect rock below. Accordingly, many parties prefer to rappel after the best climbing instead of scrambling broken rock to the summit.

Face climbs currently are rare on the Tower, but cracks abound—cracks that are uniquely consistent in quality. The perfection and length of these remarkable fissures strike most climbers as pure delight; others find the repetitive moves tedious. At times, stemming between columns adds the diversity of burning calves to the pain of toe-jams and the numbness of pumped-out forearms. The unrelenting nature gives Tower ratings a notoriously stiff reputation. A gorgeous handcrack might be rated "only" 5.9, but might well be that hard for 165 feet straight!

Because the easiest way up the rock is 5.6, all descents are by rappel. The park service has established three superb rappel routes off the Meadows, which serve as the standard descents from the summit. All require two 150-foot ropes. Many routes at the Tower (but not the Durrance) require 165-foot ropes to reach established belay stations.

ENVIRONMENT   The Tower remains sacred to Native Americans, who come to this natural shrine for religious ceremonies. To them, climbing the Tower is roughly as sacrilegious as scaling the faces at Mount Rushmore would be for other Americans. Native Americans sometimes leave prayer bundles or other offerings behind rocks or in trees; it is unlawful and disrespectful to disturb these offerings in any way. Native Americans also object to shouting and curses emanating from the cliffs while they are conducting their ceremonies. As this book goes to press, many climbers are avoiding the Tower during the month of June as a compromise toward Native American sensiblilites.

The Indians lost their homelands around the Tower after the U.S. Army and cattle ranchers arrived in the mid-1800s. The area's broad, grassy valleys and wooded hills attracted hordes of homesteaders, and the dramatic Tower served as a landmark for settler get-togethers. Today, it teams with the Black Hills of South Dakota, like twin stars, to pull vast numbers of vacationers out of the open Midwest spaces.

All these tourists can exert a significant impact on Tower climbers. Nowhere in America—Yosemite included—are climbers so inundated with questions and comments. The rangers hold frequent climbing-equipment demonstrations, and even sell a booklet entitled *How Do They Get Their Ropes Up There?* Many climbers soon learn to hide their gear in packs, rather than subject themselves to the barrage of naive questions.

CLIMBING HISTORY   According to Indian lore, the first ascent of Devils Tower occurred when seven Indian maidens jumped onto a low rock to escape a pursuing grizzly bear. They prayed to the rock to save them, and it promptly grew to its present height. The vertical cracks are said to be claw marks left by the angry bear, while the seven maidens took their heavenly place as the Pleiades star formation.

Once adventurous frontiersmen gathered at the base of the Tower, they eventually devised a way to climb it. Two ranchers drove wooden stakes into a crack, forming a crude ladder up the sheer South Face. They saved their final summit bid until a huge Fourth of July celebration in 1893, when they planted the American flag on the summit to the cheers of the throng below. Several dozen people climbed the Tower via this ladder until 1927, when the lower 100 feet was removed because it had deteriorated. The upper section was left for its historical significance, and can still be seen near the Walt Bailey route.

The first rock climbers scrabbled up the *Wiessner Crack* in 1937; its 5.7 squeeze chimney was then one of the hardest climbs in the country. The *Durrance Route*, climbed the next year, is technically easier (5.6) and has since become the most popular way up the Tower. During this early period, climbing permission was granted by park service headquarters in Washington D.C.; the bureaucratic hassle, combined with the Tower's remote location, limited ascents until the late 1950s. The most celebrated climb came in 1941, when a parachutist landed on the summit and was rescued by climbers five days later. In 1983, an unknown individual climbed the Tower and dived off with a parachute, thus completing the jump 42 years later.

The *Durrance* and *Wiessner* were the only routes on the Tower until 1951. In 1956, climbers celebrated the national monument's 50th anniversary by putting up several new routes, mostly nail-ups by army teams. Many of these early climbs have long been forgotten, though occasional "new routes" still run across rusted army ring-angle pitons.

The '60s brought a few free climbs, but artificial climbs still predominated. During the '70s, however, climbers from Colorado and elsewhere pushed the new free-climbing standards onto the Tower, eliminating the aid on classic lines like *Hollywood & Vine* and *McCarthy–North Face*. By the early 1980s, dozens of routes up to 5.12 fell to more climbers than ever. While many thousands of people have reached the summit, the majority still use the *Durrance Route*.

A few difficult bolted face climbs appeared during the later '80s, but the most significant recent changes include new fixed rappel routes from the Meadows, and several well-marked approach trails built to minimize impact by all the vertical traffic.

CAMPING   A busy campground inside the monument next to the Belle Fourche River charges $10 per site. Private pay campgrounds are also available nearby. Clustered around the monument entrance, one can find small grocery stores, a gas station, showers and laundries. Elsewhere, free camping is difficult to find, because local ranchers don't take kindly to trespassers. The monument charges an entrance fee of $4 weekly per vehicle; Golden Eagle passes are accepted.

SEASONS AND WEATHER   The main climbing season is April through October. From April through May, one can expect highs to be in the 60s and lows in the low 40s; rainfall is modest and climbing weather is generally very dependable. June through August the highs are in the 90s and the lows in the 50s; there's not much rain and you can climb nearly all the time. September and October feature perfect low 70s as the highs, dropping into the low 40s at night; rainfall is low and the climbing is ideal.

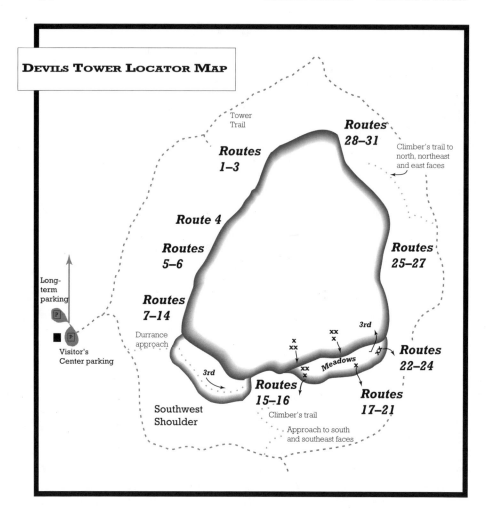

DEVILS TOWER LOCATOR MAP

Tower
Trail

Routes
28–31

Routes
1–3

Climber's trail to
north, northeast
and east faces

Route 4

Routes
5–6

Routes
25–27

Long-
term
parking

P

Routes
7–14

Visitor's
Center parking

Durrance
approach

3rd

xx
x

3rd

x
xx

xx
x

Meadows

x

Routes
22–24

Southwest
Shoulder

3rd

Routes
15–16

Climber's trail

Routes
17–21

Approach to south
and southeast faces

Summer midday heat on the south face can make the rock too hot to touch, and has been known to pan-fry climbers' brains. By climbing on the shady or sunny side of the Tower, as appropriate, temperatures can usually be kept comfortable year-round.

RESTRICTIONS AND WARNINGS Climbers should park in the long-term lot, which also offers precious shade. All climbers must register in the visitors center before and after climbing each day. Camping is allowed in the campground only—no summit or cliffside bivouacs. The use of power drills or pitons, leaving fixed ropes unattended, leaving pets at the base of climbs, and throwing anything off the Tower are all prohibited. Foot traffic has severely eroded the summit plateau; protect shrubs and wildflowers by walking on rocks. The south face is prone to rockfall; hard hats are recommended. Watch out for rattlesnakes, spiny plants and the occasional falcon attack. It is unlawful to disturb Native American prayer bundles in any way.

GUIDEBOOKS *Devils Tower National Monument: A Climber's Guide*, (1995) by Richard Guilmette, Renee Carrier and Steve Gardiner. Exhaustive treatment of Tower routes, history and general information. Available from climbing shops or through the Devils Tower Natural History Association, PO Box 37, Devils Tower, WY 82714.

A Poorperson's Guidebook: Free Climbs of Devils Tower (revised almost annually) by Dennis Horning and Hollis Mariott. Covers routes in detailed topo format, but has no history or first-ascent information. Available locally at the visitor center or from Dennis Horning, RR 1 Box 88-Y, Custer, SD 57730.

GUIDE SERVICES AND EQUIPMENT Local guide service is provided by Tower Guides, located at the entrance to the monument (307-467-5589 or 970-325-4879 in winter or http://www.climbnet.com/towerguides). They also sell climbing gear and rent shoes. The nearest full-service equipment stores are Wheeler Dealer in Gillette, Wyoming and Mountain Goat Sports in Rapid City, South Dakota.

EMERGENCY SERVICES In case of emergency, contact a park ranger to coordinate rescues and ambulances. The nearest hospital is 28 miles away: Crook County Memorial Hospital, 7130 AK, Sundance; (307)283-3501.

GETTING THERE Inexplicably, no public transportation serves this particular national monument.

DEVILS TOWER WEST FACE

10 Tulgey Wood (10a)
11 McCarthy West Face Variation
      (10c)
12 El Matador (10d/11a)
13 Digital Extraction (12–)
14 Rangers Are People,
      Too/Direct Southwest (11b)

WEST FACE

1 **Carol's Crack (11a)** Extra medium Stoppers. FA: Bob Yoho, Chick Holtkamp, Carol Black and Jeff Baird, 1978.

2 **Approaching Lavender (11c)** Thin stemming; tiny wires to medium Stoppers. FA: Paul Piana, Bob Cowan, Todd Skinner and Beth Wald, 1984.

3 **One-Way Sunset (10d/11a)** Extra small to large Stoppers and a couple of large nuts to 4"+ for upper pitches. FA: Dennis Horning and Jim Slichter, 1977.

4 **Risque (12)** Sharp bolted arête left of Bonzo; Quickdraws. FA: Todd Skinner, Beth Wald, Bill Hatcher and Jim Schlinkmann, 1985.

5 **No Holds for Bonzo (10d/11a)** Left side of pillar, excellent fingerlocks. FA: Mateo Pee Pee and Jim Schlinkmann, 1985.

6 **Bloodguard (12a)** Desperate tips crack; medium Stoppers, small wires. FFA: Todd Skinner, Beth Wald, Bob Cowan and Paul Piana, 1984.

7 **Brokedown Palace (12a)** Rarely repeated. Many small wires and medium Stoppers. FA: Bruce Price and Mike LaLone, 1973. FFA: Mark Sonnenfeld and Steve Hong, 1981.

8 **Jerry's Kids (10b)** Popular left-facing corner; three bolts. FA: Jim Schlinkmann, Mateo Pee Pee and Barney Fisher, 1985.

9 **Mr. Clean (11a or 10 C1)** Sustained fingers/thin hands; start at yellow roof with bolt. Extra medium to large Stoppers, large nuts to 4". FA: Curt Haire and Dennis Horning, 1976. FFA: Henry Barber and Chip Lee, 1977.

10 **Tulgey Wood (10a)** Gorgeous left-facing corner; extra Stoppers, 2"to 3½"nuts. FA: Mark Hesse and Dan McClure, 1972.

11 **McCarthy West Face Variation (10c)** Extra medium-large Stoppers. FA: Chris Ballinger, Dennis Horning and Steve Gardiner, 1978.

12 **El Matador (10d/11a)** Continuous height-dependent stemming. Extra Stoppers all sizes. FA: Bob Yoho and Chick Holtkamp, 1978.

13 **Digital Extraction (12–)** Classic thin fingers, strenuous, sustained. Many small-medium wires, three #1 and two #3 Friends, large nuts for top. FFA: Steve Hong and Mark Sonnenfeld, 1982.

14 **Rangers Are People, Too/Direct Southwest (11b)** Link-up of two perfect cracks; 5.9 corner, then wild wide fingers. FA: Unknown.

DEVILS TOWER WEST FACE

1   Carol's Crack (11a)
2   Approaching Lavender (11c)
3   One-Way Sunset (10b)
4   Risque (12)
5   No Holds for Bonzo (10d/11a)
6   Bloodguard (12a)
7   Brokedown Palace (12a)
8   Jerry's Kids (10b)
9   Mr. Clean (11a or 10 C1)
10 Tulgey Wood (10a)

SOUTH FACE
Photo on pages 18-19.

15   **Durrance (6)**   Tower's easiest, most popular route. Short pitches, wide cracks. Large nuts, extra slings for fixed pegs. FA: Jack Durrance and Harrison Butterworth, 1938.

16   **Weissner (7)**   Tower's first technical climb. Squeeze chimney; large nuts and tube chocks. FA: Fritz Weissner, William House and Lawrence Coveny, 1937.

17   **Bon Homme Variation (8)**   Traverse left below small roofs. Extra medium to large nuts. FA: Dennis Horning and Howard Hauck, 1972.

18   **Double Indemnity (10d/11a)**   Two cracks left of old stake ladder; traverse right to belay. FA: Steve Hong, Karin Budding and Mark Smedley, 1980.

19   **Direct Southeast (11d)**   Three cracks right of stake ladder, thin fingers. Many tiny to small Stoppers. FA: Pete Ostlund and John Horn, 1965. FFA: Steve Hong, Karin Budding and Mark Smedley, 1978.

20   **Walt Bailey Memorial (9)**   Beautiful sustained hands, 165-plus feet. Extra medium Stoppers. Note: Do not rappel route—crack eats ropes. FA: Gary Cole, Ray Jacquot and Charles Blackmon, 1959. FFA: Scott Woodruff and Jeff Overton, 1974.

21   **Hollywood and Vine (10c)**   Utter purity of line; extra small nuts. FA: Ray Jacquot and Gary Cole, 1959. FFA: Scott Woodruff and Jeff Overton, 1974.

EAST FACE
Photo on pages 20-21.

22   **Soler (9–)**   Tower's first aid line up perfect corner. Hanging belay; extra medium nuts. FA: Anton Soler, Art Lembeck, Herb Conn and Ray Moore, 1951. FFA: Layton Kor and Ray Jacquot, 1959.

23   **TAD (7)**   Popular handslot two cracks right of Soler. Extra medium to 4" nuts. FA: Dave Gallagher and Jack Morehead, 1956. FFA: Dan Burgette and Charles Bare, 1973.

24   **El Cracko Diablo (8)**   Fine hands/offwidth, hanging belay to right; extra medium to 4". FA: Rod Johnson and Pat Padden, 1973.

25   **Casper College (10+)**   Thin bulge; extra small to medium Stoppers. FA: Dud McReynolds, David Sturdevant, Walt Bailey and Bruce Smith, 1956. FFA: Dennis Horning and Jim Beyer, 1977.

26   **Burning Daylight (10b)**   Finger jams through roof; extra medium Stoppers. FA: Mike Todd and Dennis Horning, 1977.

NORTH FACE
Photo on pages 22-23.

27   **Belle Fourche Buttress (10–)**   Sustained, fingery; extra medium Stoppers. FA: Don Ryan and Gary Cole, 1961. FFA: Dennis Horning and Dave Rasmussen, 1977.

28   **Patent Pending (8+)**   Offwidths, roof, shady choice for hot days. Extra large nuts to 4", optional tube chocks. FA: Charles Bare and Jim Olsen, 1971. FFA: Bruce Bright and Dennis Drayna, 1972.

29   **New Wave (10a)**   Brilliant link-up to Assemblyline; avoids 180-foot 5.4 bushwhack. FA: Unknown.

30   **Assemblyline (9)**   Lo-o-o-ng handcrack. Extra medium nuts to 3". FA: Dennis Horning and Judd Jennerjahn, 1975.

31   **McCarthy North Face (11a or 5.7 C2)**   Wild, varied, wonderful; many medium to large Stoppers. Bolted face just right, *McCarthy's Brother*, is 5.10a. FA: Jim McCarthy and John Rupley, 1957. FFA: Dennis Horning and Frank Sanders, 1978.

The Meadows

3rd

old stake ladder   5.11   5.10

5.9

5.11

165 ft.   4th

5.3

3rd

19

20   21

17   18

approach

22   24

**DEVILS TOWER
SOUTH FACE**

15 *Durrance (6)*
16 *Weissner (7)*
17 *Bon Homme Variation (8)*
18 *Double Indemnity (10d/11a)*
19 *Direct Southeast (11d)*
20 *Walt Bailey Memorial (9)*
21 *Hollywood and Vine (10c)*

**DEVILS TOWER
EAST FACE**

21 Hollywood and Vine (10c)
22 Soler (9–)
23 TAD (7)
24 El Cracko Diablo (8)
25 Casper College (10+)
26 Burning Daylight (10b)
27 Belle Fourche Buttress (10–)

DEVILS TOWER NORTH FACE

27 Belle Fourche Buttress (10–)
28 Patent Pending (8+)
29 New Wave (10a)
30 Assemblyline (9)
31 McCarthy North Face (11a or
    5.7 C2)

24

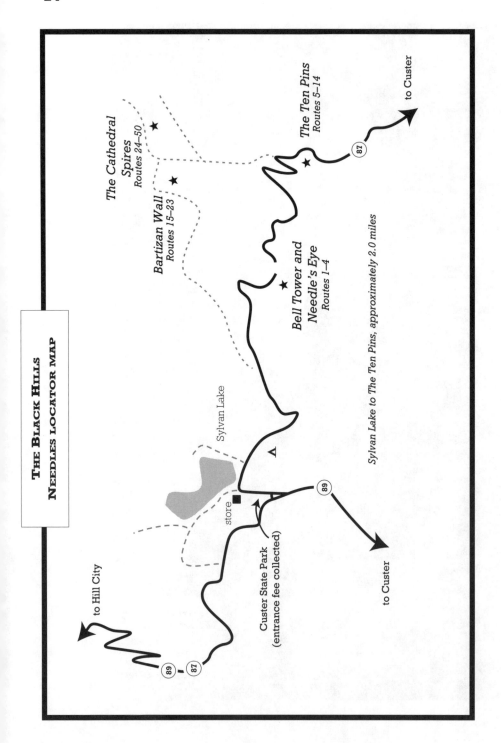

THE BLACK HILLS
NEEDLES LOCATOR MAP

to Hill City

89

87

Sylvan Lake

store

Custer State Park
(entrance fee collected)

89

to Custer

Sylvan Lake to The Ten Pins, approximately 2.0 miles

Bell Tower and
Needle's Eye
Routes 1–4

The Cathedral
Spires
Routes 24–50

Bartizan Wall
Routes 15–23

The Ten Pins
Routes 5–14

87

to Custer

SECTION TWO

THE BLACK HILLS, SOUTH DAKOTA

NEEDLES AND MOUNT RUSHMORE

The surprisingly lush Black Hills host a 20-mile swath of incredible outcrops, with well-developed climbing areas at either end and hundreds of rarely-scaled backcountry spires in between.

To the south lies the Needles, a jumble of almost comically pointed towers. Their granite is so coarse-grained that sometimes people actually tie off individual crystals for protection. The prospect of a leader fall on this cheese-grater rock can be thoroughly unnerving, thanks especially to the intimidating runouts demanded by the Needles' strict traditional ethics.

If scanty protection isn't a favorite diet, head north through the Black Hills to the more recently developed Mt. Rushmore area, where the crags have been sprinkled with liberally bolted sport-climbing routes. Ample camping is available within walking distance of either area, though climbers must compete for tent space with hordes of other tourists who visit this historically rich, beautiful region.

CLIMBING   No popular climbing area in North America holds anything approaching the quantity of granite spines poking out of the Black Hills' backbone. Though some Needles and Rushmore towers reach up to 400 feet high, the sharper ones average a single pitch; the larger ones are typically blockier and less pointed. Approaches can be as short as stepping out of the car or as "long" as a mile's walk on gentle terrain. The actual climbing at the two areas is fairly similar, though the atmospheres differ radically.

Needles—Needles climbing is decidedly unusual and not everyone enjoys it. The gigantic crystals look—and feel—very different from the granite most climbers know. The rock is generally sound; even precarious-looking projecting crystals are usually solid. Cracks are rare, though lines of crystals and sharp knobs supply delightful face holds over unlikely-looking blank sections. The technical difficulty usually depends on the size and spacing of available crystals.

The definitive difficulty of Needles climbing is largely psychological. The runouts here can be frightening and stem from a long tradition of only protecting free and on the lead. New hard routes are often better protected, as certain locals have developed to an amazing degree the art of drilling while standing on little nothings. Modern protection devices reduce the seriousness of some leads, as can tying off projecting crystals. The sketchy protection frightens many climbers away from the Needles, but there's a simple remedy: Instead of attacking at your limit, enjoy a truly wild route three grades lower. Then, work back up the grades according to taste and experience.

A third unique difficulty of some Needles climbs doesn't start until one reaches the top: Where natural rappel horns aren't available, the traditional descent involves simul-rapping—a nerve-racking, rope-wrecking exercise best learned from a skilled practitioner. In short, one partner raps off by using the other as a counterweight! Lately, locals have placed discreet permanent rap anchors on popular routes. Summit registers still grace most of the Needles. Please enjoy reading the old entries and adding new ones, but don't remove these vital markers or anything inside them; they maintain an essential historical continuity for the area.

Rushmore—Mount Rushmore doesn't worry its climbers with terminal runouts or bizarre simul-raps. It's a burgeoning sport-climbing venue where the emphasis centers on enjoying the delights of crystal-crimping while securely clipped to bombproof bolts. The most treacherous things a climber encounters here are hordes of motor homes and overloaded minivans with occupants gaping at the famous faces of the Mount Rushmore National Memorial.

Rushmore rock is similar to that of the Needles, though perhaps not as distinctively shaped. The crags are spectacular nonetheless: The routes follow crystals, knobs and devious dikes up great leaning fins or lumps of seamless granite.

ENVIRONMENT   The Black Hills defy any stereotyped image of South Dakota. Though surrounded by flat wheat and cornfields, the Black Hills are rolling, forested and exquisitely beautiful. The pine forests hold small, clear streams and occasional reservoirs.

The Needles are part of Custer State Park, which includes a game preserve for herds of bison, elk and pronghorn antelope. Like nearby Devils Tower, roadside climbing here is plagued by tourists, especially at the Needle's Eye area. The gawkers often can't (or won't) understand that answering their shouted questions is less important than negotiating the crux runout. Fair warning: Climb at the Needle's Eye only in good humor and in the early morning or evening.

Outside of the park boundaries, travelers confront the most amazing concentration of tourist traps anyone could wish to avoid. Two million sightseers flock here every year to gawk at the gigantic faces of U.S. presidents carved into Mount Rushmore, the world's largest man-made work of art. Many a climber has stood in the tourist throngs, picking an imaginary line over Lincoln's forehead on what is also certainly the planet's largest collection of chiseled (though strictly forbidden) routes.

But a nearby monument looms even larger and more interesting because it's still being carved, in large part by a long-time Needles climber/demolition engineer. The massive Crazy Horse Monument is also one of the few tributes to Native Americans in this land of General Custer. Badlands National Park, about 50 miles further east, is another don't-miss attraction. A desolate moonscape of dry, sedimentary canyon mazes, the Badlands couldn't possibly present a greater contrast to the lushness of the Black Hills.

CLIMBING HISTORY The earliest climbing explorations in the Needles began in the 1930s with the Wiessner Route on Inner Outlet. During the late 1940s and 1950s, one energetic couple made more than 200 first ascents, most of them to virgin summits. By the 1960s, a few Midwesterners, Northeasterners and Californians made regular midsummer visits to the Needles. Since these characters climbed at the top of contemporary standards, and because of their bold climbing style, some of their routes still see very few repeats.

Even though they pushed to the maximum—reason enough for many

ROBERT FINLEY LEADING *EL MATADOR* (5.10D/11A). PHOTO BY BOB GAINES.

to relax their ethics—Needles climbers maintained a rigid tradition of placing protection (including the occasional bolt) free and on the lead. They dismissed any spire ascended with aid as "not yet climbed."

During the 1970s, ever-increasing numbers of locals and outsiders dispatched the few remaining virgin summits and put up many more hard climbs. Most of the early activists faded away, while an increasingly mobile climbing community moved in, or rather, passed through. By the early '80s, climbers traveled great distances to join the Needles' raucous annual "Climb-a-Thon" celebrations, as topropes festooned the spires and kegs flowed freely. As the '80s faded, so did that tradition.

Meanwhile, just a few miles up the road at Mount Rushmore, another Needles tradition was being hammered—or more accurately, drilled—to pieces. A faction of locals disgruntled with ironclad ground-up Needles ethics began developing Rushmore quietly. Not surprisingly, heated arguments arose over "proper" style. Eventually the traditionalists retreated to the Needles and rap-bolting prevailed at Rushmore.

Bolstered by abundant bolted protection, Rushmore standards almost immediately outstripped the Needles, despite that area's long history of hard, bold routes. Unfortunately, the freewheeling sport climbers soon drew the critical eye of Rushmore Memorial rangers concerned with maintaining some level of decorum. To their credit, locals banded together to work with the rangers rather than against them, organizing cleanups and helping to establish designated trails to minimize overall impact.

Now, the memorial accepts climbers as an important "user group," and climbers from all over the world brave the snarls of tourist traffic to wrestle with gymnastic free climbs on dozens of gorgeous, readily accessible crags.

And the Black Hills' backcountry holds untold opportunities for compelling new lines. Roughly midway along the Black Hills spine between Needles and Rushmore lies what we know as Harney Peak, and what the Plains Indians called "The Center Of The Universe." Climbing these backcountry crags gives a heady taste of the undeniable intrinsic power hereabouts.

SEASONS AND WEATHER   The normal climbing season runs from July through October, with rainfall the principal limiting factor earlier in the year. July and August high temperatures are typically in the upper 70s and lows are in the 40s; there's a low to moderate risk of rain, and plenty of good climbing days. September and October temperatures drop to highs in the lower 50s and lows in the chilly 30s. But there isn't much rain and the climbing is pretty good. November through March is chilly, with highs in the 30s and lows in the 20s; rainfall is moderate and some climbing gets

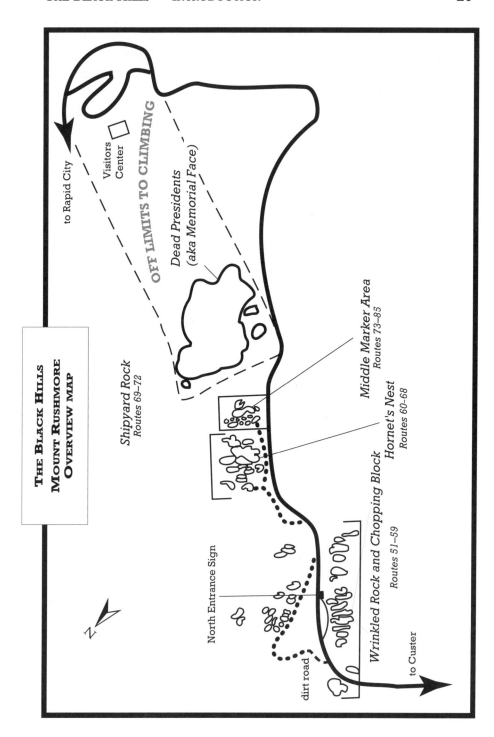

THE BLACK HILLS
MOUNT RUSHMORE
OVERVIEW MAP

to Rapid City

Visitors
Center

OFF LIMITS TO CLIMBING

Dead Presidents
(aka Memorial Face)

Shipyard Rock
Routes 69–72

Middle Marker Area
Routes 73–85

Hornet's Nest
Routes 60–68

Wrinkled Rock and Chopping Block
Routes 51–59

North Entrance Sign

dirt road

to Custer

N

done. April and June feature highs in the 50s, lows in the 30s, but there's a good bet that it will rain, so it's risky to count on good climbing.

Some summers stay wet for long periods, while some winters offer good, albeit chilly, climbing weather; 50-degree days are not uncommon in winter. Rushmore is about 1,000 feet lower than Needles, so it stays warmer in off-season and hotter in summer. Either way, one can pick shady or sun-warmed faces to suit the day.

CAMPING   *Needles*—Ample camping options exist around the Needles, but most popular with climbers is the Sylvan Lake Campground ($8-10), with the excellent bouldering just a half-mile away. From here, one can reach the principal cliffs on foot, though most lazy climbers drive. Entry requires a South Dakota Parks entrance license of $6 for five days or $12 for an annual pass, sold right at the gate. Showers are available and the little general store and restaurant at Sylvan Lake are open in summer. Nearest laundry is in Custer. Numerous private campgrounds are available within a short drive. Also, in the national forest outside of Custer State Park, one can scout out free out-of-the-way camping spots, but fires are prohibited.

Rushmore—The area is peppered with standard national forest campgrounds. Climbers tend to gravitate toward the free, primitive-style sites at Windy Point and Horsethief Lake, near the memorial's north entrance and a few minutes' walk from the crags. Fires are allowed only on established fire grates in the campgrounds and not at all on open national forest lands. Please cooperate with these simple restrictions to ensure continued access to this free-camping bonanza. Nearest towns are Keystone and Hill City.

RESTRICTIONS AND WARNINGS   *Needles*—Beyond a ban on power drills, Custer State Park imposes no restrictions on climbing, except that if climbers continue to create a spectacle (i.e., cause traffic jams) in the Needle's Eye area, it may be closed to climbing. Otherwise, be prepared to downclimb if a runout seems too long. Some older bolts require thin carabiners.

Rushmore—Climbing is strictly forbidden in a well-marked zone around the Rushmore Memorial faces. Violations here could endanger continued access to the rest of Rushmore. Climbers should register at the memorial's visitor center or at the sign-in kiosk near the north entrance; the more the rangers see and hear from climbers, the more they'll support the activity. Dogs, bicycles and boom boxes are prohibited off-road in the memorial, which includes the main Rushmore cliffs. The memorial bans power drills, though hand-drilling on rappel is accepted. Note: To preserve future climbing access near the memorial and discourage illegal climbing, any first ascent information of Mount Rushmore itself has been excluded at the suggestion of the local climbing community.

GUIDEBOOKS   *Touch the Sky: The Needles in the Black Hills of South Dakota*, (1983) by Paul Piana. Great history and detailed verbal descriptions. Available at outdoor shops or by mail from Bob Archbold, Box 655, Rapid City SD 57709. Also from the American Alpine Club, 710 Tenth Street, Suite 100, Golden, CO 80401.

A Poorperson's Guidebook: Selected Free Climbs of the Black Hills Needles, (1989) by Dingus McGee and the Last Pioneer Woman. Available locally or from Dennis Horning, Poorperson's Guidebooks, 808 South 4th, Laramie, WY 82070, ($4 mail order). Contains no historical information or photos, but is cheap and functional.

El-Cheep-O Topo Guide to Mount Rushmore, (1989) by Mike Lewis. Available ($2) from Rockwalk, PO Box 254, Custer, SD 57730. Short and to the point, but good maps to the formations and access trails.

Mount Rushmore National Memorial Climber's Guide (self-published 1996) by long-time activist Vern Phinney is now available. Contact the author at Box 2336, Rapid City, SD 57709.

GUIDE SERVICES AND EQUIPMENT   Local guide services include Reach For the Sky Mountaineering (605-343-2344), Sylvan Rocks Climbing Adventures (605-574-2425) and Mountain Mania (605-343-6596 or 605-343-1970). Guides are also available from Tower Guides at Devils Tower (307-467-5589 or 970-325-4879 in winter, http://www.climbnet.com/towerguides). The nearest equipment stores are in Rapid City: Mountain Goat Sports, 2111 Jackson Blvd and Sports World, in the Baker Park Shopping Center.

EMERGENCY SERVICES   *Needles*—In case of emergency, contact a Custer park ranger or call Custer County Sheriff at (605)643-4467. The nearest hospital is the Custer Community Hospital located next to the clinic at 1041 Montgomery, Custer, telephone hospital: (605)673-2229, clinic: (605)673-2201.

Rushmore—Contact a memorial ranger for any emergency.

GETTING THERE   Trailways buses leave daily (in the morning) from Rapid City to Custer. Air and bus transportation serve Rapid City, from which you can rent a car. Hitchhiking, even from Custer, is not likely to be very efficient, but once one finally reaches the Rushmore Memorial or Sylvan Lake, walking to the cliffs is easy.

NEEDLES ROUTES

BELL TOWER AND NEEDLE'S EYE

Note: Please stay off Routes 1 and 2 when many tourists are present. Two ropes are needed for rappels from all routes.

BELL TOWER AND NEEDLE'S EYE

1	Unnamed (8)
2	Unnamed (10b)

1   **Unnamed (8)**
Start downhill and climb up as if going into the "eye," then traverse right to edge and gain flake. Serious runout on second pitch! FA: Rich Goldstone and Don Storjohann, 1964.

2   **Unnamed (10b)**
Good pro with small nuts; controversial bolt may have been removed. FA: Renn Fenton, year unknown.

3   **Every Which Way But Loose (10)**
FA: Pete deLanoy, Paul Muehl, Paul Piana, Mark Smedley, 1979.

4   **Kamp's Crack (10)**
FA: Bob Kamps, Rich Goldstone, 1967.

BELL TOWER
AND NEEDLE'S
EYE

| 3 | *Every Which Way But Loose* (10) |
| 4 | *Kamp's Crack* (10) |

2 ropes

5.10

fp

crack

5.10

blocks

THE TEN PINS
From uphill

5   **Energy Crisis (11)**   Deception Pinnacle. FA: Kevin Bein and Barbara Devine, 1980.

6   **End Pin (10+)**   Corner nearest road, two bolts. FA: Roger Wiegand and Pete Cleveland, 1970. FFA: Rich Goldstone and Dick Williams, 1975.

7   **Quartz Jester (10 or 11+)**   FA: Henry Barber and Dennis Horning, 1978. Direct variation: Kevin Bein, 1981.

8   **Kingpin (8/9)**   Climb the line of least resistance. This was originally 5.7, before the hold broke. FA: Herb Conn and Jan Conn, 1952.

9   **Queenpin (9 or 10–)**   FA: Royal Robbins, Liz Robbins, Dick Laptad and Sue Prince, 1964.

From downhill

10   **Tricouni Nail (Cerberus) (8)**   Superb route. FA: Royal Robbins, Liz Robbins, Dick Laptad and Sue Prince, 1964.

11   **Superpin (10)**   Runout. Rock may be less good than on other pins; crystals have broken. FA: Henry Barber, Dennis Horning and Chip Lee, 1977. FA of spire (via no pro 5.11): Pete Cleveland, 1967.

12   **Tent Peg (7)**   FA: Royal Robbins and Liz Robbins, 1964.

13   **Safety Pin (6)**   FA: John Gill, Bob Kamps, 1967.

14   **Hairy Pin (10+)**   Only one bolt below shoulder; there is 15-plus feet of 5.10 past bolt, then more hard climbing. Serious runout! FA: Pete Cleveland, 1967.

THE TEN PINS FROM DOWNHILL

9   Queenpin (9 or 10-)
10   Tricouni Nail (Cerberus) (8)
12   Tent Peg (7)
13   Safety Pin (6)
14   Hairy Pin (10+)

BARTIZAN WALL

15 **The Naked Rib (10)**   All bolt pro. First pitch is runout 5.10;
second pitch is 5.9, only one bolt. FA: Paul Muehl, Pete deLanoy,
1982.

16 **Crack of Earthly Delights (9)**   Descent: Make a 30-foot rap to the
west, then stem north and scramble down. FA: Jim Black, Pete
deLanoy and John Matteson, 1980.

17 **Terror-Cracktyl (9)**   FA: Steve Levin, Jim Black, Bob Archbold
and Rich Cordes, 1980.

18 **Angry Morning (9)**   FA: Bob Archbold and Jim Black, 1980.

19 **Thanatos (12–)**   FA: Kevin Bein, Sam Slater, Jim Waugh and
Bruce Thompson, 1980.

20 **Window of the West (11–)**   FA: Sam Slater and Bruce Thompson,
1980.

21 **Bartizan (Kevizan) (10+)**   FA: Steve Wunsch and John Bragg,
1977.

22 **Elrod's Epic (9)**   FA: Bob Archbold and Elrod Williams, 1981.

23 **Afternoon Delight (7)**   FA: Bob Archbold, Jay Ellwein and Todd
Van Alstyne, 1980.

THE CATHEDRAL SPIRES

Note: Routes may appear on several different photos.

24 **Friend of the Devil (8)**   Climb through bomb bay chimney to
small ledge with fixed piton, face climb right to crack and route 25.
FA: Pete deLanoy, Bob Archbold and Brian Sarni, 1980.

25 **Unnamed (9)**   FA: John Gill, 1964.

26 **Unnamed (5)**   The fingercrack right of chimney offers better
climbing and pro. FA: Herb Conn and Jan Conn, 1952.

27 **God's Own Drunk (8+)**   The large dihedral on Khayyám Spire.
FA: Howie Richardson, Jim Kanzler and an Englishman, 1971.

28 **Moving Finger (3)**   FA: Herb Conn and Jan Conn, 1953.

29 **Tower of Darkness (3)**   FA: Herb Conn and Jan Conn, 1953.

30 **Unnamed (8)**   FA: Herb Conn and Jan Conn, 1952.

31 **Paradise Enow (10+)**   FA: Paul Muehl, Tom Young and Dave
Hashisaki, 1981.

32 **Blue-Eyed Siberian Husky (9)**   Starts next crack left of *Possibly
Not.* FA: Bob Archbold and Mark Ebel, 1978.

33 **Possibly Not (7)**   5.8 if started by *Blue-Eyed Siberian Husky*
crack. FA: Brian Sarni, Bob Archbold and John Driscoll, 1979.

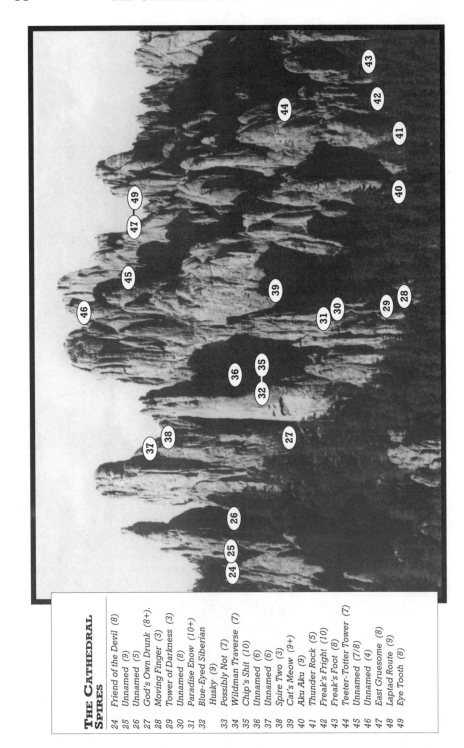

THE CATHEDRAL SPIRES

24 Friend of the Devil (8)
25 Unnamed (9)
26 Unnamed (5)
27 God's Own Drunk (8+).
28 Moving Finger (3)
29 Tower of Darkness (3)
30 Unnamed (8)
31 Paradise Enow (10+)
32 Blue-Eyed Siberian
    Husky (9)
33 Possibly Not (7)
34 Wildman Traverse (7)
35 Chip's Shit (10)
36 Unnamed (6)
37 Unnamed (6)
38 Spire Two (3)
39 Cat's Meow (9+)
40 Aku Aku (9)
41 Thunder Rock (5)
42 Freak's Fright (10)
43 Freak's Foot (8)
44 Teeter-Totter Tower (7)
45 Unnamed (7/8)
46 Unnamed (4)
47 East Gruesome (8)
48 Laptad Route (9)
49 Eye Tooth (8)

34 **Wildman Traverse (7)**   FA: Paul Piana, Ken Jones and Chris Field, 1971.

35 **Chip's Shit (10)** FA: Bob Archbold and Chip Devereaux, 1979.

36 **Unnamed (6)** Runout on easier rock. FA: John Dudra and Fred Beckey, 1952. FFA: Herb Conn and Jan Conn.

37 **Unnamed (6)** Climb crack to top. FA: Barry Corbet, Jake Breitenbach, Charles Plummer, 1956.

38 **Spire Two (3)** May be line taken by Bill House, Fritz Wiessner and Lawrence Coveney in 1937—first of the Cathedral Spires to be climbed. FA: Herb Conn, Jan Conn, 1949.

39 **Cat's Meow (9+)** Last pitch is approximate: follow seam of crystals past bolt to crack. FA: Bob Archbold and Todd Van Alstyne, 1980.

40 **Aku Aku (9)**   FA: Dick Laptad and Sue Prince, 1965. FFA: Mark Powell, Dave Rearick and Bob Kamps, 1966.

2 ropes

5.5

no pro

5.6

2 ropes

36

27

UPHILL FROM KHAYYÁM SPIRE

27   *God's Own Drunk (8+).*
36   *Unnamed (6)*

41   **Thunder Rock** (5)   FA: Herb Conn, Jan Conn and Chuck Nauman, 1953.

42   **Freak's Fright** (10) FA: Bob Kamps and Rich Goldstone, 1967.

43   **Freak's Foot** (8)   FA: Mark Powell, Beverly Powell and Bob Kamps, 1966.

44   **Teeter–Totter Tower** (7)   FA: Herb Conn and Jan Conn, 1954.

45   **Unnamed** (7/8) Requires thin carabiners to fit old-style bolt hangers. FA: Herb Conn and Jan Conn, 1953.

46   **Unnamed** (4)   Begin at back of wide chimney. FA: Herb Conn, Jan Conn, 1948.

47   **East Gruesome** (8) Guidebooks traditionally have not described this fine, intricate route, which was put up in tennis shoes with a 50-foot rope. FA: Herb Conn and Jan Conn, 1959.

48   **Laptad Route** (9)   FA: Dick Laptad, Paul Muehl, Dave Emery and Julie McFarland, 1979.

49   **Eye Tooth** (8)   FA: Bob Kamps, Mark Powell and Beverly Powell, 1962.

50   **Unnamed** (9)   FA: Mark Powell, Beverly Powell and Bob Kamps, 1964.

x   bolt location approximate

5.10

2 fp

42

42   Freak's Fright (10)

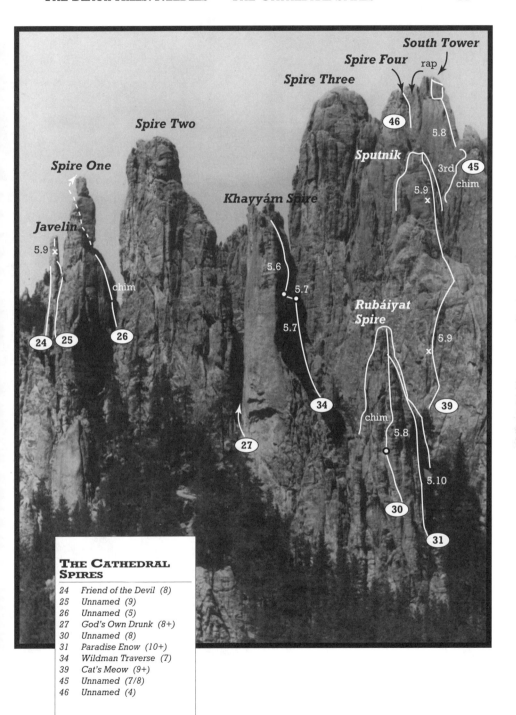

South Tower

Spire Four rap

Spire Three

Spire Two

Spire One

Javelin

5.9

Khayyám Spire

46

5.8

Sputnik

3rd 45

chim

5.9

5.6

5.7

chim

5.7

Rubáiyat Spire

5.9

24 25 26

34

27

chim

5.8

39

5.10

30

31

THE CATHEDRAL SPIRES

Gruesome Twosome

East

48

Spire Five

Empire State Building

5.7

5.6

Teeter-Totter Tower

Freak's Foot

44

50

Aku Aku

Thunder Rock Freak's Fright

5.8

X
X
X
X

Flying Buttress

40

41

42

43

THE CATHEDRAL SPIRES

40	Aku Aku (9)
41	Thunder Rock (5)
42	Freak's Fright (10)
43	Freak's Foot (8)
44	Teeter-Totter Tower (7)
48	Laptad Route (9)
50	Unnamed (9)

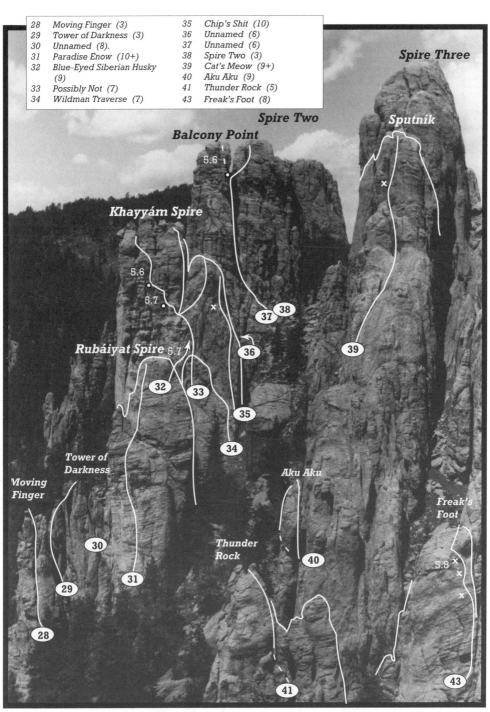

28	Moving Finger (3)	35	Chip's Shit (10)
29	Tower of Darkness (3)	36	Unnamed (6)
30	Unnamed (8).	37	Unnamed (6)
31	Paradise Enow (10+)	38	Spire Two (3)
32	Blue-Eyed Siberian Husky	39	Cat's Meow (9+)
	(9)	40	Aku Aku (9)
33	Possibly Not (7)	41	Thunder Rock (5)
34	Wildman Traverse (7)	43	Freak's Foot (8)

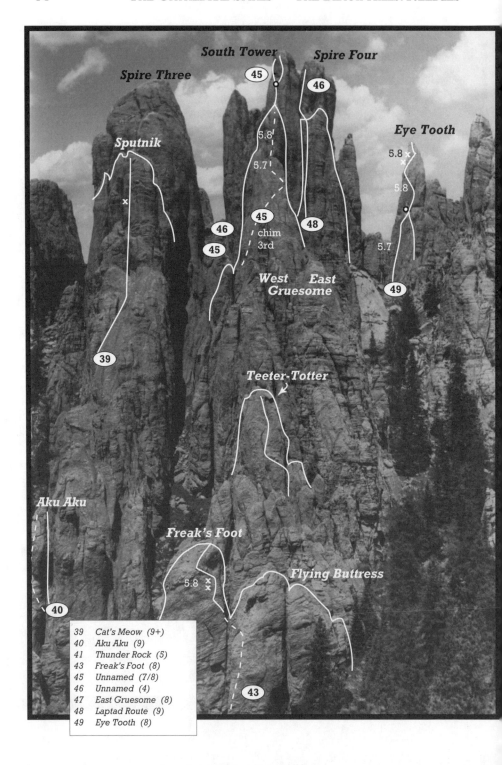

South Tower

Spire Four

Spire Three

45

46

Eye Tooth

Sputnik

5.8

5.8

5.7

5.8

46

45

45
chim
3rd

48

5.7

39

West
Gruesome

East

49

Teeter-Totter

Aku Aku

Freak's Foot

Flying Buttress

40

5.8

39   Cat's Meow (9+)
40   Aku Aku (9)
41   Thunder Rock (5)
43   Freak's Foot (8)
45   Unnamed (7/8)
46   Unnamed (4)
47   East Gruesome (8)
48   Laptad Route (9)
49   Eye Tooth (8)

43

CLIMBERS ON THE TENT
PEG. PHOTO BY BOB
GAINES.

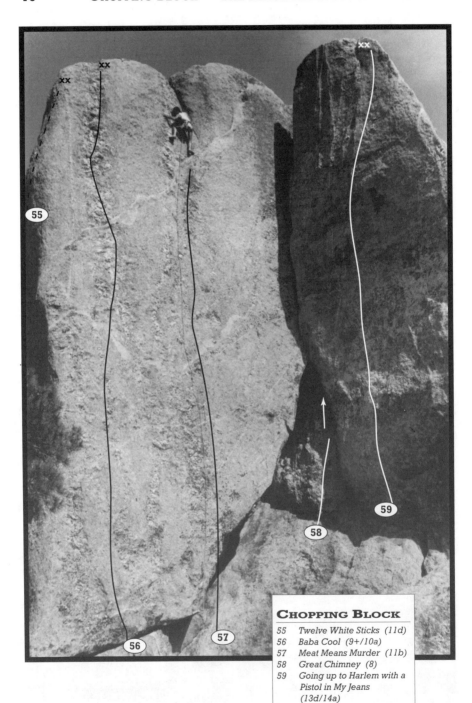

CHOPPING BLOCK

55 Twelve White Sticks (11d)
56 Baba Cool (9+/10a)
57 Meat Means Murder (11b)
58 Great Chimney (8)
59 Going up to Harlem with a
    Pistol in My Jeans
    (13d/14a)

MOUNT RUSHMORE ROUTES

For more information, see the introduction to The Black Hills on page 25.

WRINKLED ROCK

51   Tomcat Tracer (13a)   Desperate deadpoints.

52   Double Chin (11c)   Need a long sling on first bolt.

53   Oh, Sheri! (11c)   Dicey mantel.

54   Wrinkle in Time (11c)   Devious diagonal dike.

CHOPPING BLOCK

55   Twelve White Sticks (11d)   Stunning arête.

56   Baba Cool (9+/10a)   Line of fat crystals.

57   Meat Means Murder (11b)   Line of not-so-fat crystals.

58   Great Chimney (8)   Need large nuts.

59   Going up to Harlem with a Pistol in My Jeans (13d/14a)   Heinously thin face, height-dependent.

**HORNET'S NEST—
EAST SIDE**

60   Iron Butterfly (12c/d)
61   Mothra (13a)
62   Beetlejuice (12b)

HORNET'S NEST— EAST SIDE

60   Iron Butterfly (12c/d)   Go up wide, polished stripe.

61   Mothra (13a)   Continuous face up thin stripe.

62   Beetlejuice (12b)   Face just left of arête.

HORNET'S NEST— WEST SIDE

63   Yuppie Warfare (12a)

64   Critical Crewcut (12c)   Air time is virtually certain.

65   Mr. Critical (11b/c)   Rushmore's first rap-bolted route.

66   Mr. Critical Direct Finish (11a) "Easy" way out.

67   Critical Finish (12a)   For that full-body pump.

68   Lonesome Cowboy (12a/b) Start in crack, then go right to face.

SHIPYARD ROCK—WEST SIDE

69   Tsunami (aka Waves) (8)   Starts on west face.

70   Not–So–Sweet (6)   Offwidth flake.

71   Nutrasweet (11b)   Many thin mantels.

72   Boxcars and Airplanes (6)   Mini-spire.

MIDDLE MARKER AREA

73   Stardancer (8)   Fantastic bolted face.

74   Jupiter Fly–By (10b)   Thin water groove, easy runout to top.

75   Saturn Boogie (9+)   Short face, pinnacle.

76   Borealis Strut (9)   Short tower.

77   Thin Edge (7 R)   No pro above the first bolt.

78   Pluto's Playground (10a)   Simul-rap descent!

79   Dark Side (9)   Crack/face.

80   Moonstone (10 R)   Cool, if a little scary.

81   Morning Ecstacy (8)   Bolts to a long 5.4 runout.

82   Lost in the Mire (9)   Thin seams, tricky pro, 5.4 runout.

83   Little Dripper (10b)   Small pro.

84   Big Dripper (9)   Medium wires/TCUs.

85   Weird Water (7)   Go up the trough, or 5.10 direct start.

MIDDLE MARKER AREA (RIGHT)
73   Stardancer (8)
74   Jupiter Fly-By (10b)
75   Saturn Boogie (9+)
76   Borealis Strut (9)
77   Thin Edge (7 R)
78   Pluto's Playground (10a)
79   Dark Side (9)
80   Moonstone (10 R)
81   Morning Ecstacy (8)
82   Lost in the Mire (9)
83   Little Dripper (10b)
84   Big Dripper (9)
85   Weird Water (7)

INDEX

Bolded numbers refer to photos of the feature or route. Formations and areas are in all captials.

Access: It's everybody's concern

the**ACCESS FUND**

The Access Fund, a national, non-profit climbers' organization, is working to keep you climbing. The Access Fund helps preserve access and protect the environment by providing funds for land acquisitions and climber support facilities, financing scientific studies, publishing educational materials promoting low-impact climbing, and providing start-up money, legal counsel and other resources to local climbers' coalitions.

Climbers can help preserve access by being responsible users of climbing areas. Here are some practical ways to support climbing:

- **COMMIT YOURSELF TO "LEAVING NO TRACE."** Pick up litter around campgrounds and the crags. Let your actions inspire others.

- **DISPOSE OF HUMAN WASTE PROPERLY.** Use toilets whenever possible. If none are available, choose a spot at least 50 meters from any water source. Dig a hole 6 inches (15 cm) deep, and bury your waste in it. *Always pack out toilet paper* in a Ziploc™-type bag.

- **UTILIZE EXISTING TRAILS.** Avoid cutting switchbacks and trampling vegetation.

- **USE DISCRETION WHEN PLACING BOLTS AND OTHER "FIXED" PROTECTION.** Camouflage all anchors with rock-colored paint. Use chains for rappel stations, or leave rock-colored webbing.

- **RESPECT RESTRICTIONS THAT PROTECT NATURAL RESOURCES AND CULTURAL ARTIFACTS.** Appropriate restrictions can include prohibition of climbing around Indian rock art, pioneer inscriptions, and on certain formations during raptor nesting season. Power drills are illegal in wilderness areas. *Never chisel or sculpt holds in rock on public lands, unless it is expressly allowed* – no other practice so seriously threatens our sport.

- **PARK IN DESIGNATED AREAS,** not in undeveloped, vegetated areas. Carpool to the crags!

- **MAINTAIN A LOW PROFILE.** Other people have the same right to undisturbed enjoyment of natural areas as do you.

- **RESPECT PRIVATE PROPERTY.** Don't trespass in order to climb.

- **JOIN OR FORM A GROUP TO DEAL WITH ACCESS ISSUES IN YOUR AREA.** Consider clean-ups, trail building or maintenance, or other "goodwill" projects.

- **JOIN THE ACCESS FUND.** To become a member, *simply make a donation (tax-deductible) of any amount.* Only by working together can we preserve the diverse American climbing experience.

The Access Fund. Preserving America's diverse climbing resources.
The Access Fund • P.O. Box 17010 • Boulder, CO 80308